First published in the UK by Sweet Cherry Publishing Limited, 2024
Unit 36, Vulcan House, Vulcan Road,
Leicester, LE5 3EF, United Kingdom

Nauschgasse 4/3/2 POB 1017
Vienna, WI 1220, Austria

2 4 6 8 10 9 7 5 3 1

ISBN: 978-1-80263-095-4

Football Rising Stars: Sophia Smith

Text by Harry Meredith
Illustrations by Sophie Jones

www.sweetcherrypublishing.com

Printed and bound in India

SOPHIA SMITH

THE UNOFFICIAL STORY

Written by

HARRY MEREDITH

Sweet Cherry

CONTENTS

1

COLORADO HOMECOMING

Thousands of fans filled Dick's Sporting Goods Park football stadium in Colorado, USA, in anticipation of a national team match. The USA were facing off against Columbia, a fierce and competitive South American side.

Both teams would be supported by loyal and excited fans, but nobody in the stadium was quite as excited as one of the players on the pitch. Sophia Smith, a forward for the USA, was returning home. Having grown up in Colorado, it was a dream come true for Sophia to play for her country in her home state. All of her friends, family and coaches would be watching her, and she wanted to make them incredibly proud.

The game was a friendly, which meant that neither side were

competing for points or progression. Instead, they were there to test themselves against another nation in preparation for future tournaments, to try out ideas and see what worked and what didn't. However, no match would ever be that simple against the USA.

At the time, the USA national women's team were ranked as number one in the world. Not only did the team want to win, but more often than not, they were *expected* to. With a large pool of talented players, there was always a pressure on the team to perform to the best of their abilities. Each player was constantly competing to keep their spot in the team. They had to prove to everyone that they deserved to play in the next match and in international tournaments in the future. Some players can let this pressure get to them, but the best take it as a challenge – playing with confidence and the same level of excitement they felt as a child.

 As the players emerged from the tunnel and walked out onto the pitch,

Sophia felt ready to give her all for her nation and for her supporters. The thousands of fans in attendance cheered as their heroes prepared to start the game. The USA players wore a red and navy kit, with rainbow detailing on their numbers in honour of Pride Month, and Columbia wore their usual bright yellow. The referee blew her whistle and the game began.

The USA started the match strongly, but a resolute Colombian defence kept them well at bay.

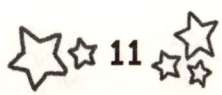

Chances fell to both sides, predominantly to the hosts, as they searched for the opening goal. Sophia was playing with bursts of energy and determination, chasing after every loose ball, committing to each tackle and making lots of runs in search of a goal.

Sophia's persistent runs eventually paid off with a chance in the 54th minute. Rose Lavelle, a tenacious midfielder, won a duel for the ball in the centre of the pitch and broke forward. Spotting Sophia's run, she passed a precise through ball to the rushing forward, between a static defence. The defenders were unable to do anything as Sophia collected the ball and raced through on goal. With the defenders chasing her, the goalkeeper rushing off her line to meet her and the space closing, Sophia had to act quickly. Running at an incredibly fast speed, Sophia took a shot with her left foot. She tumbled to the ground and watched as the ball flew towards the goal. Although her strike hit the goalkeeper's leg, it was only a small deflection. The ball

rose into the air, but not high enough to go over the crossbar, and nestled into the back of the net. Sophia had scored! Her teammates ran over to her and hugged her in celebration. Sophia's family and friends, alongside all of the fans in the stadium, leapt into the air and cheered. The star forward had scored on her homecoming and given her nation the lead in the friendly!

For some players, this would be more than enough. But instead of extinguishing Sophia's enthusiasm, her goal made her even more determined to perform well. Only a few minutes later, Sophia found another golden opportunity. Once again, Lavelle was a thorn in the Colombian team's side. With so many Columbian players high up the pitch desperately in search of an equaliser, she easily stole the ball in the centre of the pitch and created the perfect chance for a counter-attack. Sophia sprinted towards the penalty box and Lavelle found her with a pinpoint pass. Between the defenders, Sophia controlled the ball, looked up and calmly slotted it past the outstretched arms of the goalkeeper. The USA had a 2-0 lead, and Sophia had scored her second goal of the match in front of her home support. She had always dreamt of helping her team to victory, and as a forward she was always thinking of putting the ball in the back of the net. The feeling was unlike anything else. Sophia had done herself, her country and her family proud. She was playing exactly like the star striker that she was.

USA debutant Taylor Kornieck finished the scoring by adding a third goal in the closing stages of the match. The final whistle was blown, and Sophia and her teammates could enjoy a job well done. Not wanting the incredible day to end, Sophia was one of the last to leave the pitch. She stayed until the very end so that she could celebrate the moment with her friends and family, taking in every second of one of the best days of her career to date.

2

HOOPS OR GOALPOSTS?

Football, or 'soccer' as it is known
in the USA, is far from the country's
most popular sport. Instead, millions
choose to play American football,
hockey, baseball or basketball. Sophia
Smith was born into a family who

couldn't get enough of hoops, free throws and slam dunks. Her father had been a basketball player for the University of Wyoming, and he passed his love for the sport onto his three daughters. Being a sporty family, the Smith girls also played other sports too. Sophia's older sisters, Gabrielle and Savannah, introduced her to the game of football, often playing kickabouts with her in the back garden. And they quickly noticed that their little sister had a knack for the game.

At four years old, Sophia was far too young to consider a future in the sport, or to even be aware that she had a natural talent for it. She played simply because she enjoyed it. Football was the perfect opportunity to run around,

 make tackles, score goals and have fun. It was in kindergarten (the US equivalent to reception) where Sophia met some friends who also played. One of those friends was Jaelin Howell, who would eventually go on to play

for the US women's national team – just like Sophia!

When the parents of one of the girls decided to start a recreational local football team, Sophia and her friends jumped at the chance to join the newly-formed Timnath Twisters. Sophia now had a safe and fun environment to play and learn in, where she could socialise with her friends and release all of her energy. She could make mistakes, learn from them and constantly improve her game.

One of the moments
that made Sophia love
football even more was
when the women's national team
came to town. The Smiths were
unable to get tickets for the highly
anticipated match, but the team
held a separate event where fans
could meet the players. Sophia and
her family waited in line for what
seemed like forever, but it was more
than worth it when Sophia was able
to meet her idols. She even had a
picture taken with the USA's all-
time leading goalscorer in women's

football, Abby Wambach. Seven-year-old Sophia treasured the photo, and sometimes she'd look at it and dream of playing for her country too.

It didn't take long for Sophia to stand out from the crowd. Even at such a young age, it was clear that she had something different. The moment she stepped onto a football pitch, she caught the eye of any bystander and captivated them. Sophia was a player who demanded attention just from her understanding and expression of the sport. As a result of this, Sophia was

invited to join another team called
Arsenal Colorado. It was a step up
in competition, but they were still a
local football team not too far from
home.

Sophia might have grown up in a
basketball family, and she still played
basketball from time to time, but
there was no denying that football
was her game. And not only that,
but she was exceptionally good at it.
Everyone around her could see it.

3

THE ROAD TO DENVER

Sophia had been developing year after year, at a pace far greater than her teammates, so once again she was considering her next opportunity. While she was still at Arsenal Colorado, around the age of twelve,

Sophia became known to Lorne Donaldson – one of the top football youth coaches in the state. Impressed by his outstanding reputation, Sophia's parents met with the coach to see if there was a place for Sophia in his side. It was a perfect match, and it was decided that Sophia would join one of the top football programmes in Colorado: Real Colorado. As Sophia's coach, Donaldson would strive to get the best out of the developing star.

While at first this may appear to have been an

easy decision, that was far from the truth. Although Sophia was always looking for opportunities to improve and test herself against the very best, playing for Real Colorado was going to come with sacrifices. The team was based in the centre of Denver, which was an hour and a half away from Sophia's home. Getting to practice every day was going to be difficult, but Sophia's mother was determined to make it work. She decided to quit her job and find something that would fit around Sophia's new schedule.

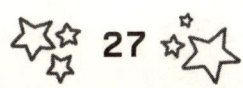

Every day after school, she made the three-hour round trip to Denver and back for her daughter. Sometimes, if the traffic was bad or they didn't leave on time, the journey on its worst days could even take four hours total. Sophia was incredibly grateful for the sacrifices her parents made for her. To pay them back, she was going to make the most of her chance.

With time now limited, Sophia would often have to do some of her homework in the car to and from training. If she didn't, she'd have to do it late at night after an exhausting day at school and an equally exhausting training session. Yet Sophia wouldn't have traded her schedule for the world. More than anyone, Sophia was determined to make the most of her opportunity. Like a professional, Sophia stuck to her routine, eager to learn every day. Her dedication and willingness to practise even helped the coaches improve. Inspired by Sophia and her family's sacrifices, they packed as much into the sessions as they could.

If Sophia missed a shot in the previous match, even if it was just *one* missed attempt, she'd want to immediately learn how to correct it,

requesting that chance in training again and again to ensure that she'd score next time. She loved hearing the *swish* of the rippling net as the ball was fired into it, and the incomparable feeling of delight when she celebrated a goal.

Sophia and the coaches' hard work paid off, with the team often defeating their opponents and putting in strong

performances during tournaments.
Before long, just as the emerging
teenager was finding success
in her home state, her talents
were gradually becoming known
nationwide. Scouts for the national
team had started to pay attention to
the rising star from Colorado.

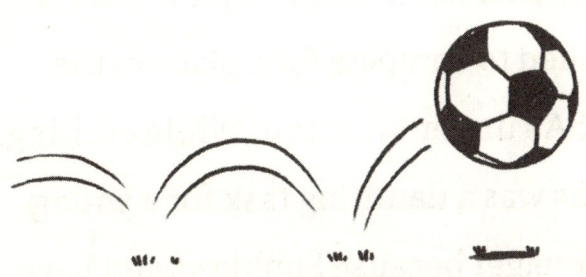

4

USA YOUTH

At the age of thirteen, the young forward was invited to her first national team camp. Sophia had been called to compete for a place in the USA's under 14s setup. While exciting, this was a daunting task for a young teenager because Sophia would have to leave home and face lots of new challenges alone.

Yet she was never really alone. Sophia quickly made friends at camps and was always surrounded by friendly and talented players. Not to mention some of the country's best coaches focussing on improving her game and nurturing her talent.

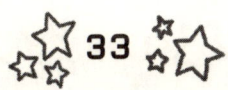

Sophia fitted in well with her teammates and for the most part was a crucial player in national team camps. One time when she wasn't selected, Sophia was devastated.

It meant the world to her to play for her national team. But instead of dwelling on this disappointment, Sophia got right back to her feet and pushed herself to improve, wanting to ensure that she was selected for the next camp. And it wasn't long before she was called up once again. Sophia's dedication, work ethic and talent was always going to shine through. No matter any dip in form or missed shot, Sophia simply had abilities that could not be ignored by anyone.

As the most successful country in women's football at the time, the USA maintained high expectations for upcoming talent. They were constantly looking ahead – sometimes many years ahead – trying to craft and build squads that could continue their winning legacy. But this also came with added pressures, competition and expectations. Sophia never let any of this get to her, as her family had instilled a strong confidence in her. She had an unwavering belief that

she had what it took to make it all the way.

This combination of natural ability, hard work and confidence eventually led to an opportunity that most sixteen-year-olds could hardly imagine in their wildest dreams. Sophia was invited to go and train with the USA national team! Not in any of the youth setups or reserves, but with the idols she had grown up watching on a screen. She would get the chance to meet, train and play with some of the best

female football players in the world –
players who were known worldwide
as tremendous athletes and sporting
heroes in their own right.

Sophia celebrated the news with
her friends and family. She was
delighted to be given such a unique
opportunity, but she would be lying
if she said she wasn't nervous.
She refused to allow herself to be
overcome by the situation and
planned on being entirely focussed
when the time came, learning from
and contributing to the team during
drills and sessions.

Although Wambach was now retired, there were so many other stars who Sophia was able to meet and train with. There was Carli Lloyd, Julie Ertz, Alyssa Naeher, Crystal Dunn and Alex Morgan – global football superstars who were now Sophia's teammates. Sophia was welcomed into the group and soon gained invaluable experience from the camp. Although she didn't make her debut while she was with the squad, she made many memories that she'd take into her future in football.

5

STANFORD UNIVERSITY

University and college sport is of enormous importance in the USA. Fans fill stadiums larger than most professional grounds, with capacities of thousands. In women's football in the US, the best players are offered

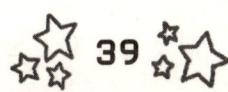

scholarships to attend colleges and then play for their team.

A scholarship is when the college or university pays the majority of the student's tuition fees because of their academic or sporting excellence. With Sophia approaching the end of her time at high school in Colorado, she had many admirers from across the country. As a teenager who had played with the US national team, almost every college programme in the country wanted her on board. Eighteen-year-old

Sophia also had the option to bypass college entirely. Many football teams would have happily added her to their squad. Sophia was a young and upcoming talent who could have broken into a professional team in the US or across the pond in Europe. Yet there was never really any doubt about what Sophia wanted to do. She wanted to play for a college for the development and experience.

While men's football is a sport filled with enormous sums of money, the same cannot be said for the

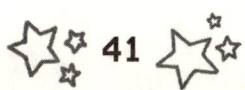

women's game. Women who play professionally often have to give much more thought to the realities of life after or around football,  because they most likely won't make life changing amounts of money during their career. However, while Sophia was considering her options, money in women's football was steadily on the way up. There were more professional players and more support than ever before. But there were still no guarantees. So, after taking advice from her family, friends and teachers, Sophia opted to go for the academic route. She wanted to set herself up with qualifications and skills that could help her off the pitch as well as on it.

Now that Sophia had made this call, there was still an important decision to make. She had to decide which scholarship offer to accept, so that she knew what the colours of her new university team would be. After some deliberation, Sophia decided to go to Stanford University. Stanford University had a long history as one of the top educational institutions in the US. Not to mention an outstanding football programme, the Stanford Cardinal, which had helped to mould and develop many football stars – such as Kelley O'Hara, Christen Press and Andi Sullivan.

This was an incredibly exciting time for Sophia. But it was also a move that came with lots of uncertainty and nervousness. She was moving across the country to California, hours away from home. She'd be miles away from family, friends and home comforts. Nonetheless, Sophia knew that this

was a move she wanted to make. She wanted to get lost in the excitement of making new friends, competing against top talent and beginning her journey to becoming a professional football player. The young forward couldn't wait to get started.

6
TOUGHEST MOMENT

Sophia made thirteen appearances for Stanford Cardinal during her debut season, scoring seven goals, the team's third highest tally, and also providing two assists. However, Sophia could have scored and played a lot more if her season had gone to plan.

In a match against Utah, in which Sophia had already scored, she found herself another opportunity. Feeling like she was going to score, Sophia charged forwards and prepared to strike, but she was hit from behind before she could follow through. A chasing defender had recklessly dived in and missed the ball, whacking Sophia and sending her tumbling to the ground. Instead of cheering in celebration of a goal, Sophia now found herself yelling out in pain on the ground.

This was unlike any pain she had ever felt before, and she could do nothing but writhe on the ground as the referee and medical assistance came to her aid. Sophia's parents were visiting for the weekend and watched on from their seats, feeling powerless and deeply concerned by the events unfolding on the pitch.

Sophia was taken out of the game and accompanied to the hospital with her parents. She knew she had done  something to her ankle and, thinking more about football than

the pain, hoped that it wasn't as serious as it felt. She had earned herself a spot in the first team, was scoring goals and felt ready to help make Stanford Cardinal's campaign a success. But the doctors at the hospital revealed the exact news she feared. Sophia had broken her ankle, tearing ligaments in the process, and her body would need months to recover. With her injury, it was unlikely that Sophia would play again this season. Lying on the hospital bed, Sophia was consoled by her family.

Her leg had been put into a cast and it was confirmed that her injury would require surgery. Fortunately, the surgery was a success and before long it was time for Sophia to focus on the next chapter: to give everything to her recovery and rehabilitation so that she could get back on a football pitch as soon as possible.

After the initial shock had subsided, Sophia was ready to put herself on the path to recovery. To avoid further complications, she took her time and gave her body and mind everything it needed to get back to feeling more like her old self. Rather than dwelling on the missed matches, she embraced a positive mindset and found little things that could make her smile. Some positives and opportunities even came from her injury. Having been in a tireless routine for years in the pursuit of her goal, Sophia was able to stop and take a breath for the first time in a long while. She was also able to make more time for her friends, family and

education, pulling herself out of the constant pursuit of excellence and allowing herself to rest.

Sophia may not have made any further appearances for Stanford Cardinal that year, but her injury was never going to stop her from progressing. She would come back to the sport more determined than ever to play football to the best of her ability.

7

RETURNING TO FOOTBALL

After a summer of recovery and catching up with her family, it was time for Sophia to return to Stanford University. After a mixed first year, Sophia was counting down the days until she could get stuck into her second year. She longed to get back

on a competitive football pitch and push herself and her team further. But Sophia's excitement also came with a dose of nerves. She had spent months building her body back to full strength, and she hoped that she was still the same football player as last year. With some injuries, players never return to their previous form. Sophia didn't like to think that way, but sometimes it was incredibly difficult to ignore those thoughts. All Sophia knew was that she'd be able to banish them sooner or later. There was no other antidote than putting her boots back on the grass and playing once again for Stanford Cardinal, testing herself against the top college athletes.

With the college season starting in August, Sophia still had some time to get stuck into her studies and work on her fitness. She enjoyed catching up with her friends from her first year and talking with them about how excited she was to get back to playing. Everyone at Stanford Cardinal couldn't wait to get started. They all felt optimistic about this

squad, and there was good reason for it. They had one of the most talented rosters around.

Finally the day came for Sophia to return. Just as it had always

been, playing football was second nature to her. She no longer needed to worry about her body. She was back to full health, playing at her best and making steps further on the field than she had ever gone before. The Stanford Cardinal enjoyed an incredibly impressive season. Teams feared playing them – Sophia and

 her teammates were unstoppable when they were at their best.

After the team progressed from their regular season games, they competed in the National Collegiate Athletic Association (NCAA) Championship (also known as the College Cup). Top college teams from across the country would be battling it out in knock-out football to be crowned as the best. Stanford Cardinal cruised through their group, overcoming Prairie View A&M, Hofstra, Penn State and BYU to earn a spot in the semi-final. This is where the competition really gets tough, as big teams with even bigger expectations clash against one another.

Stanford Cardinal had been drawn against UCLA Bruins, a tough opponent but one that they hoped to defeat. And with stars such as Sophia and Catarina Macario in their side, they had a good chance of doing just that. UCLA took an early lead with a goal from Chloe Castañeda, unsettling Stanford. But on an eighteen-match consecutive winning streak, Stanford

were going to have something to say about the final outcome of the match. Within twenty-two minutes, Sophia and her teammates flipped the script. Sophia scored two goals and Carly Malatskey scored one, making the score 3-1 in the first half. Sophia topped off an incredible day for herself and her team by grabbing a third goal – and her hat-trick – in the second half, helping her team win the match 4-1. They had progressed to the final and would get the opportunity to triumph as national champions!

If Stanford were to win, they would need to beat the historically successful North Carolina Tar Heels. The Tar Heels had won the NCAA Championship a record twenty-two times since it started, whereas Stanford Cardinal had only won the competition twice. If the team were going to succeed, they'd need all of their stars to play to the best of their ability.

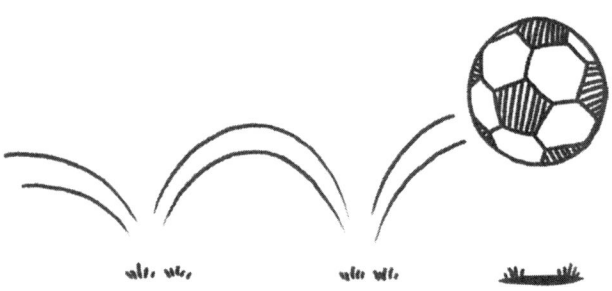

8

NATIONAL CHAMPIONSHIP

The big day finally arrived. Sophia and her teammates stepped off the coach into the warm and welcoming sunshine of San Jose, California. Sophia had her earphones in, taking in every moment but trying to remain calm and composed, ensuring that

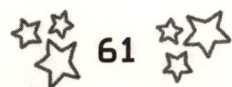

the excitement and grandeur of the day didn't distract her. She knew she had a job to do, and in order to perform, she needed full concentration.

Fans started to fill the stands of the Avaya Stadium. There were plenty of the players' family and friends in attendance to wish everyone well. Camera crews and presenters were there too, as many eyes were on the match, excited to see which team would finish the year as national champions.

The two teams walked out onto the pitch to cheers and applause. Huddling together, the players were led by their captain and team leaders in a pre-match motivational speech. Everyone was fired up for the big occasion. All of this pre-match build-up, excitement, adrenaline and desire seeped into the game. Full forced tackles were made by both sides; each and every player was determined to do their best for their team and win just one more football match.

As the sun slowly set, bright floodlights lit the pitch and the

players as they competed on their stage. The game was intense, with players engaged in defensive battles, fighting for midfield control and trying to be the first to break the deadlock and score the first goal of the match. Despite both sides' efforts, they couldn't put the ball past the two commanding goalkeepers. Sophia and her forwards were halted by a fierce defence, but the same was true for the Tar Heels' attackers. Neither side were able to score in regular or extra time, so this match was going to be decided another way: a penalty shoot-out. The two teams met with their coaching staff before the shoot-out, getting final words of wisdom from their mentors and taking a well-deserved drinks break.

Each team discussed which five players would be taking the penalties. They needed brave individuals who were ready to do their bit for the team and could ignore the pressure of taking a penalty in front of thousands, showing no fear at a time when others might want to hide away. For Sophia, as a forward who

loved to score, there was never any doubt. She wanted to be one of the five and score for Stanford Cardinal. Only months ago, Sophia had been sidelined with her broken ankle. She had dreamt about being a part of moments like this, and she was going to cherish every second.

Sophia and her teammates lined up on the halfway line. North Carolina would take the first penalty. With her arms around her teammates, Sophia could hardly watch. But there was no need to worry. Her goalkeeper, Katie

Meyer, got Stanford Cardinal off to the perfect start by brilliantly saving the opening penalty. Stanford took advantage of this by scoring their first, as Macario coolly slotted the ball into the back of the net. Rachel Jones levelled the shoot-out by scoring North Carolina's second.

Now it was time for Sophia to make the long walk to the penalty spot. Focussed, Sophia tried to shut out all of the stadium noise. Her

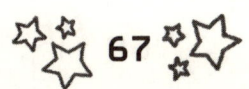 team had an advantage and she didn't want to let that slip. In a

moment that mattered, Sophia struck the ball with everything she had … and scored! Sophia jogged back to her teammates with a smile. She felt proud of herself, but there were still several penalty kicks to go. Stanford scored two of their three remaining kicks, while North Carolina were able to handle the pressure and score all three – with two of the scorers being future England Lionesses, Alessia Russo and Lotte Wubben-Moy. The two teams were locked together once more at a score of 4-4. The penalties went to sudden death, where one missed chance, one misplaced kick, can decide an entire championship. Tori Hansen stepped up for North Carolina, but Stanford's Meyer

 guessed the right way. She dived to her right and palmed the ball away. All Stanford needed to do was score the next penalty. One more precise kick of the ball and they could lift the trophy.

It was up to Kiki Pickett. The defender made her way to the

penalty spot with a steely and
fixed glare, showing no signs of
nerves. There was only one thing
on her mind and she was going
to accomplish it. Sophia watched,
clutching tightly onto her teammate's
arm. Pickett struck the ball, sending
the goalkeeper the wrong way,
and Stanford Cardinal were the
champions! Pickett ran back to her
teammates and they charged towards
her. Coaches and substitutes
sprinted onto the pitch as
the team let out relieved
and excited cheers.

Sophia had more than played her part. She had helped to lead her team to their third championship win. In only her second year, Sophia had climbed one of the toughest mountains in college football. She was an NCAA Championship winner, and a forward that every team wished they had in their squad.

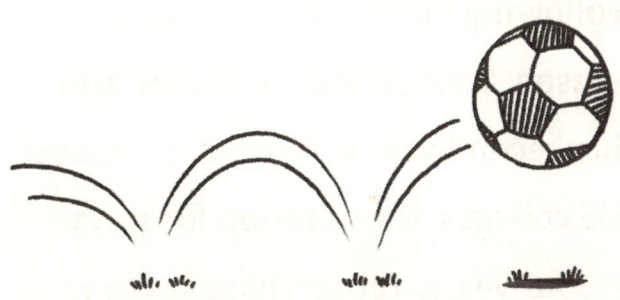

9

NWSL COLLEGE DRAFT

Following an incredibly successful season, Sophia returned home after her second year at university. In most US colleges, the duration for study is four years. Yet for those at the top

of their college sport, that duration can sometimes be cut short. If a player is over eighteen years old and opts to forego any remaining college eligibility, then they can make themselves available for the NWSL College Draft – a process where professional football teams take it in turns to select a player to join their team. The best players are always chosen in the earlier rounds and sometimes even traded for, which is when a professional team will offer money or other professional

players to get a higher draft position. Once they get a higher draft position, the team can attempt to pick their preferred player, if they haven't been selected by another team first.

As a top player who had already trained with the US national team, interest had always been high in Sophia. And since she'd displayed her talents even further throughout her college career, the interest in her had only grown. Having achieved so much during her time at Stanford,

Sophia couldn't help but question if she wanted to return for a third year. But after consulting with those close to her and going with her gut, Sophia decided to make herself available for the 2020 NWSL College Draft. It was a tough decision, because Sophia didn't want to leave her friends at Stanford behind, but she had an indescribable feeling. It felt like the right time for her to leave the comforts of college football behind and make the leap to becoming a professional player. It was time to test herself against the

very best, to challenge and compete against the top female football players in the world.

After declaring herself available, professional teams across the country had her exceptionally high in

their rankings. Sophia was seen as the star of the draft, and any teams wanting to sign her were going to need a good ranking to be in with a chance. Many rumours circled, but one team proved that they wanted her more than any other. Portland Thorns acquired the first pick of round one in

a trade with Orlando Pride, sending national team defender Emily Sonnett, along with a handful of assets, over to Orlando. The team also ended up trading to get the second pick of round one, trying to rebuild their team in style with the very best young footballers emerging from college.

For Sophia, draft night was a whirlwind. She got dressed up and prepared herself for the next step in her career. To an extent, her future was now out of her hands.

It was up to the bidding teams to see where she would play next. And Sophia certainly didn't have to wait long. She was selected as the first pick of the draft by Portland Thorns, a statement that said they believed in Sophia and thought she could be a franchise player who could lead them to future success.

After celebrating with her family in a surreal but heart-warming moment, it was time for Sophia to recognise her pick and say a few words to the Portland Thorns fans, her former teammates and all of those who had supported her throughout her college career. This was the end of one journey, but it was also the beginning of another. It was the first day of Sophia's professional football career. The newest Portland Thorns player, and first ever teenager selected, made her way onstage. Sophia stood behind the podium, with a Portland Thorns scarf hanging over her shoulders, and leant into the microphone.

'It's been a crazy past few weeks for me, but I'm so honoured and humbled to be standing here today,' Sophia began. After thanking

everyone and addressing her new fans, she ended her speech by saying: 'And finally, I want to congratulate all of the amazing young women here tonight who will see their dreams come true.'

10
PORTLAND THORNS

Now that the draft was over, it was time for Sophia to pack up her belongings and move to the northwest of the USA. She said her goodbyes to her friends, family and former teammates, before leaving to start her exciting journey in Portland, Oregon.

Sophia moved into an apartment
a short distance away from the
Portland Thorns stadium (known as
Providence Park). She was so close
to it that she could walk to training
and matches. As a coffee
connoisseur, Sophia soon
found her favourite spots
in the city and got to know
her new teammates over a hot
mug of coffee. She was joining a team
that was in the process of change,
a team trying to improve upon the
past seasons and look ahead, but
that didn't mean that the squad

wasn't already talented.
Christine Sinclair,
Canada's star striker, led
the line for the team. Not to forget
other internationally recognised
players such as Lindsey Horan,
Becky Sauerbrunn, Tobin Heath and
Adrianna Franch. With the exciting
new additions of Sophia Smith,
Morgan Weaver and Meaghan Nally,
the Portland Thorns were hoping
for an unforgettable 2020 NWSL
campaign. And Sophia and the team
certainly got that, but in a far different
manner than they would have hoped.

On the 20th of March 2020, the NWSL season was postponed indefinitely due to the COVID-19 pandemic. The majority of the world was put on hold as people stayed indoors under strict lockdowns to keep everyone safe. Sophia was gutted to be missing out on her first football season, but she understood that this was much bigger and more important than football.

The postponement lasted months, and Sophia found adjusting to this new life tough. Having moved miles away from friends and family, she was stuck in her Portland apartment alone. In a way, her time away from football due to her injury at Stanford had prepared her for a time like this. But it didn't make it any easier. Sophia missed football, she missed her friends and she missed her family. She was hoping for the day that she could break free from her isolation and return to a sense of normality.

Eventually, that day came. And while the world had changed, Sophia

was able to get back to what she knew: playing football. She was also delighted to finally see her friends and family again. While the regular season had been abandoned, the NWSL Fall Series took place towards the end of the year, and Sophia was able to play for the Portland Thorns. Revelling in her moment, it didn't take long for Sophia to fire home her first professional goal. After being substituted into a match against the Utah Royals, Sophia stunned everyone in the stadium just twenty-one minutes into her debut. She leapt up high in the box and, with no defenders around her, was able to powerfully head the ball towards goal and into the net. She celebrated wildly with her teammates as they congratulated her.

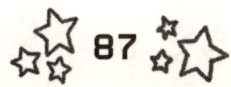

The Portland Thorns ended up finishing the Fall Series in first position. The short four-match series had been a successful start to professional football for Sophia, though it was far from the gruelling, competitive and hard-fought full

season. Sophia would truly get to test herself in a full season of professional football in the 2021 campaign, to see just how far she could take her team.

As the first pick in the draft, big things were expected from Sophia in the league. And the star from Colorado certainly didn't disappoint. Sophia made seventeen appearances and scored seven goals, helping her team finish first in the regular season standings to claim the NWSL Shield. The Portland Thorns also made it all the way to the semi-finals of the

play-offs that year. However, they were defeated by the Chicago Red Stars in an exciting but ultimately disappointing end to the season.

Sophia had got a taste of NWSL football, and she loved it. She may have had to wait, but it felt incredible to play in one of the best women's football leagues in the world. And not only that, she also got the opportunity to show that she deserved every award and appearance in the competition. She was a star player, someone deserving of the first pick in the draft and a football player who had brought success to her new team in such a short amount of time. Outsiders began to wonder just how much Sophia could accomplish.

11

USA DEBUT

Sophia's performances in the NWSL
had not gone unnoticed by the USA
national team talent scouts. During
her debut campaign with the Thorns,
she was invited to join the USA squad
and finally compete for a place in the
first team. Sophia knew she was close
to earning her USA debut and gaining

valuable minutes against the best international players in the world. She had fought long and hard for this opportunity. She had played for multiple USA youth teams, looking up to the stars in the team, patiently waiting for her chance to shine.

Sophia's national team dream came true on the 27th of November 2020. It was an unusual debut, and not quite what Sophia expected, but it was a debut she'd always cherish. The USA were playing an away match in the Netherlands – a country in Europe, several hours' flight away from the

United States. The match was also played without any fans in attendance, and with many members of staff in the ground wearing face masks. It was not the filled stadium, home soil crowd that many would dream about. But no matter what, it was an appearance for the national team. A debut playing as one of her country's best in a match against top opposition.

The USA overcame their opponents with a 0-2 victory. Goals from Lavelle and Kristie Mewis sealed the victory

for the side. The USA had come away from the match with a win but also with broken records. In the 75th minute, Sophia was substituted into the match. She ran  onto the grass with a beaming smile. She was achieving something millions of young girls dreamt of: becoming an internationally capped player for her country. Sophia also became the first player born in the 2000s to play for the USA, signalling the start of a new era for US football. In her short time on the pitch, Sophia ran as much as she could, fought for every ball and did herself and her team proud, helping the team close out the win without letting the opposition score. Sophia had enjoyed her first minutes on the pitch for the US team and she wanted more. She wanted to make sure she was a mainstay in this team for the years to come, so she went to all of the training sessions, listened to her coaches' feedback and embraced life away with the USA national team.

Sophia had performed

well, so she was invited to follow-up camps and matches where she was able to establish herself as an up-and-coming talent in the squad. Not just as an option for the future, but as a player who could make an impact for the side here and now. A talent who could help the USA win games.

On the 21st of September 2021, Sophia did exactly that in a friendly match against Paraguay. The match was played on home soil, and fans were finally allowed to be in the stadium to cheer on the teams and ramp up the atmosphere. Sophia and the team put on a show for the thousands in attendance. Sophia grabbed her first ever national team goal, the team's second on the day, in only the 6th minute of the match. Lavelle played a neat through ball to Sophia, who was charging towards goal in a blur of speed, with defenders around her. Aware of her positioning, Sophia knew she needed to take her chance. She struck the ball at goal, but it didn't fly straight into the net. A defender tried to get in the way, but all they could do was deflect its course, and the ball still crossed the line. Overcome with glee, Sophia could hardly move. She leant forward and clenched her fists and cheered. Her teammates ran to her, and the fans in attendance roared. At twenty-one years old, Sophia had scored her first goal for the USA. It was a shot and a memory that she'd never forget. And from that goal onwards, the day turned into an enormous celebration. The USA were able to put on a dominant performance in front of their cheering fans. Sophia and her teammates demolished their opponents with an 8-0 victory, showing that even in a friendly, this team meant business. They had an innate desire to win and put on a show for their fans.

After her time with the squad, Sophia returned to club action to see how far she could go with the Portland Thorns in her second full NWSL season. As Sophia left the national team camp, she thought about her future with the US squad. She was earning a regular spot and felt like a full international. But there can never be any certainties in football. Sophia had been playing for the US in friendlies and thoroughly enjoyed them, but her attention was now on the matches that mattered and doing enough to make the squad for future international tournaments. But there was still a lot of time before then, so Sophia couldn't afford to give it too much thought. All she could do was play her best for the Portland

Thorns and put on impressive performances every time her country called her up. If she played her cards right, a ticket to a major international tournament could be coming her way. Then, just maybe, she would get to compete on the biggest stage of them all.

12

NWSL CHAMPIONSHIP

Sophia took the NWSL by storm during her second full season in the league. She had helped to push her team towards success in her first season, but no one could have predicted just how well Sophia would do during the 2022 season.

The Portland Thorns were one of the toughest sides to face during that season. When the team were on form, it appeared that they could lose to no one. They kicked things off with an impressive 3-0 victory against Kansas City Current, and then they enjoyed dominant victories spread across the campaign – such as a 6-0 triumph over Orlando Pride and a 0-4 away victory against Houston Dash. But as a result of a handful of defeats and draws, the Portland Thorns were unable to reclaim their NWSL Shield. They finished in second place behind OL Reign, just one point away from retaining their trophy.

However, winning the regular season trophy in the NWSL is just the beginning. What everyone wants is to win the play-offs and be in with a chance of winning the championship game. And as a high finisher, the Portland Thorns had booked themselves a spot in the play-offs. They automatically advanced past the first round, with a home tie in the semi-finals. The fans could cheer Sophia and her teammates on as they pushed for a chance to play the championship game.

In order to progress, Sophia would need to help her side defeat San Diego Wave FC, a team based in California that was playing its first ever season in the competition. As a newly-formed side, the team was stacked with stars. On their roster was Alex Morgan, Jodie Taylor and Sophia's friend and former Stanford Cardinal teammate, Naomi Girma. But on that day, they had to put their friendship aside. They both wanted to book their team's place in the final.

San Diego Wave took the lead in the 6th minute. A headed goal from Kornieck gave Sophia and her team a lot to do. With plenty of time still left in the match, the team weren't going to give up. Cheered on by the thousands of fans in attendance, the Thorns started to fight back. In the 21st minute, Rocky Rodríguez,

 an attacking midfielder for Portland Thorns, struck an unbelievable volley

from outside the box. The sweetly struck shot fired towards goal and nestled into the top right-hand corner. It was another half-volley that sealed the match in the 93rd minute of the game. The ball bounced out to Dunn, Sophia's teammate, who sent the home crowd into delirious cheers when her effort struck the back of the net. The final minutes passed by, and it was official. Sophia and the Portland Thorns were ninety minutes away from winning it all.

In the final, the Portland Thorns lined up to take on Kansas City Current at Audi Field in Washington. Sophia was in the lineup and ready to give her all for the team, and she couldn't have dreamt of a better start to the match. In only the 4th minute, Sophia reached a through ball and was one-on-one with the goalkeeper.

In a tense moment, Sophia didn't panic. She simply rounded the goalkeeper, slotted the ball into an open net and celebrated with her teammates. An unfortunate own goal from Kansas' Addisyn Merrick sealed the tie, and Portland Thorns won the Championship game 2-0. Sophia was named as the match's MVP, which is the title given to the most valuable player on the pitch during that game.

Sophia also received further awards following the season. Having scored fourteen league goals, Sophia was the team's top goalscorer for the campaign. But it was Morgan who claimed the season's Golden

Boot award, having scored fifteen goals. However, Sophia

claimed the biggest personal prize of them all when she was named the NWSL MVP. Not just for one match, but for her performance throughout the league in that season. Sophia became the youngest ever player in NWSL history to win the award. She wasn't just ready for professional football, she had staked her claim as one of the best, if not *the* best, in the entire competition.

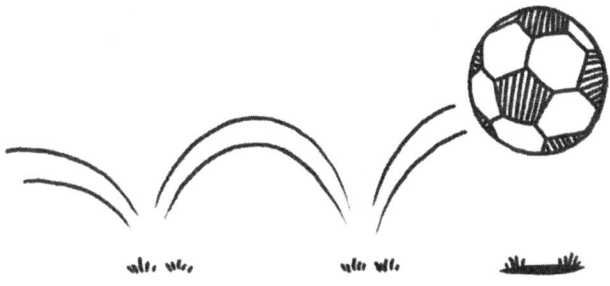

13
WORLD CUP 2023

Sophia continued her streak of good form into the 2023 NWSL season. However, this season was quite different to her others. This year was a World Cup year! In the middle of the season, national team players would have to depart, joining their country to compete in the competition.

As the league MVP for the previous season, many expected Sophia to make her first major international tournament roster. Yet nothing is guaranteed in football, and with many talented players to pick from Sophia couldn't be certain until closer to the time. After a lot of waiting, Sophia was informed that she had been selected to represent the USA in the 2023 World Cup! The team would be flying out to the distant lands of Australia and New

Zealand, in an attempt to achieve something that has never been done before: winning the World Cup three tournaments in a row. The USA had won the biggest trophy in international football in 2015 and 2019. Could Sophia help the side complete a hat-trick of wins?

The team flew out to their destination ahead of the competition so that they could adjust to the new time zones. But after the sightseeing, rest and training had been completed, it was time for

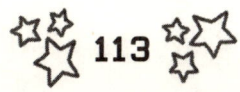

Sophia and her teammates to get stuck into action and prove that this team were at their best.

Placed in Group E, the USA would be facing off against Vietnam, the Netherlands and Portugal – teams with talented players, but ultimately a group that the USA were likely to emerge from. As the number one ranked country in the world in women's football, the pressure started to build. But in the opening match against Vietnam for the USA, Sophia helped relieve that pressure and get the team off to a brilliant start.

The match took place in front of over 40,000 fans at Eden Park in Auckland, New Zealand. The USA showed their strength by overcoming their opponents with a 3-0 win. Sophia scored the first two goals of the game, and Horan scored the final goal of the match. Sophia showed that she was not fazed by the occasion by getting her first ever major international goals and pushing her country to securing three points.

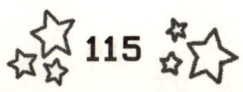

While the USA's opening match was an easy win, the same could not be said for the second and third matches. They drew against the Netherlands 1-1 and were held to a  tough 0-0 stalemate against Portugal. Fortunately, this was enough for the USA to come second in their group and progress. It was a far cry from the dominant performances the USA had shown in previous tournaments. Many US stars from those squads had now retired, and it was the turn of a new crop of players to wear the shirt and do their country proud. But with such high standards, perfection isn't always possible. Sometimes luck just doesn't go your way.

The USA were drawn against Sweden in the round of 16 – a knock-out round. The Swedes had started the tournament in red hot form by winning all three of their group matches, and now they were hoping to eliminate the tournament favourites. Used to this kind of pressure, the USA were not going to let themselves get distracted. If they wanted to win, the team needed to improve in order to make it past such a tough opponent.

Both sides threatened each other's goals in a tense ninety minutes, yet it was the USA who were coming out on top. Sophia and her teammates had lots of attempts at goal, but the Swedish goalkeeper, Zećira Mušović, produced one of the best performances of her life. No matter what the USA threw at her, the goalkeeper had an answer. And after regular time, plus extra time, neither side had found the back of the net. The match needed to be decided by a penalty shoot-out.

The teams took it in turns to take their shots. It was a far from perfect penalty shoot-out, with both sides missing attempts. However, with the score at 3-2 to the USA and only two takers to go, Sophia's penalty could decide the entire match. If she scored, she would send the USA through to the next round. Sophia took a deep breath and stepped back. She walked up to the ball, struck it and ...

 she missed. Her shot flew into the crowd behind the goal. In front of thousands of fans and millions watching across the world, Sophia wanted the ground to swallow her whole. She made her way back to her teammates, where she was consoled. She had achieved so much in her career, scored so many goals and won so many trophies. One missed penalty was not going to change that. But in the moment, Sophia couldn't think of anything else. She replayed her effort again and again in her

mind, trying to understand what went wrong.

Sweden equalised the shoot-out and sent the game to sudden death. After a missed attempt by the USA, Sweden had the chance to win it all. Lina Hurtig had the responsibility for her country. She took the strike. Naeher was able to get her glove to the ball, but it had just enough backspin to fall towards the goal. Scrambling backwards, Naeher pushed the ball off the line and away from goal. It was so tight that no one knew what had just happened. Hurtig looked to the referee, as did Naeher. Sophia and her teammates stood on the halfway line with their fingers crossed, hoping that the ball had not passed the line. Goal-line technology was used to check, and the information was passed onto the referee. She signalled with her hands that the game was over. By a millimetre, the ball had crossed the white line. It was a goal. The US goalkeeper stood in the penalty box with the ball under her arm, shocked to her core about what had just

happened. The entire US team were in disbelief, and some were in tears. Sophia couldn't believe it. The USA had been knocked out of the World Cup.

14

LOOKING FORWARD

At twenty-three years old, Sophia has achieved a lot in football. She has won the NWSL Shield and play-offs, represented her team in the World Cup and scored over fifty career goals for club and country along the way.

Although her first major international tournament didn't go as planned, Sophia is still proud of everything she has accomplished. Despite being a dominant force in women's football, the USA cannot win every single time. Football is a game that involves talent, but it is also one that involves a little bit of luck and circumstance – no matter how hard anyone plays. It is a sport where sometimes giants must fall so that new heroes can emerge.

Still at the start of her career, there is a great deal more football for Sophia to play. There are going to be other major tournaments, more league campaigns and plenty of opportunities for Sophia to display her ability. She has come so far from the young girl discovering her love for football in a backyard in Colorado, playing and laughing with her sisters, competing for her local club. Making it to the professional standard, where millions dream of reaching but often fall short, is an incredible achievement. Sophia has made a life for herself where she is surrounded by family, friends and football. And she wouldn't trade it for the world. Becoming a league MVP at the start of her career and a World Cup goalscorer in her early twenties is just the beginning, and it's exciting to think about what heights Sophia can reach. She can show the world just how tall a girl from Colorado with dreams can stand, paving the way for other

young girls with the same dream. Sophia has showed that with hard work, professionalism and positivity, anything is possible.